Clifton Park, New York 12065

Max Planck:

Revolutionary Physicist

by Jane Weir

Science Contributor
Sally Ride Science
Science Consultant
Michael E. Kopecky, Science Educator

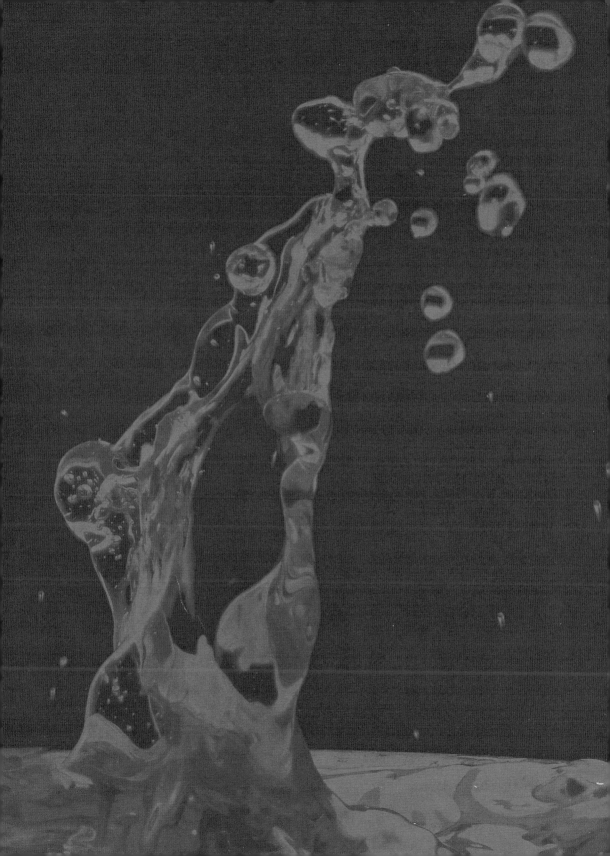

First hardcover edition published in 2009 by
Compass Point Books
151 Good Counsel Drive
P.O. Box 669
Mankato, MN 56002-0669

Editor: Jennifer VanVoorst
Designer: Heidi Thompson
Editorial Contributor: Sue Vander Hook

Art Director: LuAnn Ascheman-Adams
Creative Director: Joe Ewest
Editorial Director: Nick Healy
Managing Editor: Catherine Neitge

 This book was manufactured with paper containing at least 10 percent post-consumer waste.

Library of Congress Cataloging-in-Publication Data
Weir, Jane, 1976–
  Max Planck : revolutionary physicist / by Jane Weir
  p. cm. — (Mission: Science)
  Includes index.
  ISBN 978-0-7565-4073-9 (library binding)
1. Planck, Max, 1858–1947. 2. Physicists—Germany (West)—Biography.
3. Physics—Germany—History. I. Title.
  QC16.P6W45 2009
  530.092—dc22
  [B]   2008037622

Visit Compass Point Books on the Internet at *www.compasspointbooks.com*
or e-mail your request to *custserv@compasspointbooks.com*

Table of Contents

The End of Science?

Max Planck is one of the most important scientists of the 20th century. But when he was a teenager, people thought all the questions about science had been answered. In fact, one of Planck's college professors told him there was no point in studying science. The professor said, "In this field, almost everything is already discovered. ... All that remains is to fill a few holes." He advised Planck to study math instead.

But Planck insisted on studying science—even if he only learned about old discoveries. In particular, he wanted to understand physics—how matter and energy interact. Planck did go on to study physics in college, earning a doctorate, the highest college degree offered. But in time he would do so much more.

Planck would make discoveries and develop theories about Earth and the universe. He would bring new understanding to heat, light, gravity, and more. His ideas would become some of the most basic principles in the field of physics. Planck became most well known for his quantum theory—ideas about atoms and subatomic particles, tiny pieces smaller than an atom. His theory about these tiny particles would lay the foundation for a new branch of science called quantum physics.

Max Planck as a young man

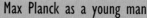

PRIX NOBEL DE PHYSIQUE 1914

LUDWIG ERNST KARL MAX PLANCK

...LIQUE DE CÔTE D'IVOIRE

VASARHELYI

Planck's research revealed new worlds in science for others to study.

In 1918, Max Planck won the Nobel Prize for his discovery of quanta. He became world famous and known as the father of quantum physics.

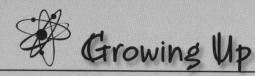

Max Karl Ernst Ludwig Planck was born on April 23, 1858, in Kiel, Germany. He was the sixth child in the Planck household. His parents, Johann and Emma Planck, gave him every opportunity to study and learn. They taught him to think for himself and work hard.

Max's relatives were very intelligent, hardworking people. His father, grandfather, and great-grandfather were college professors, and his uncle was a judge. Learning was an important part of Max's life.

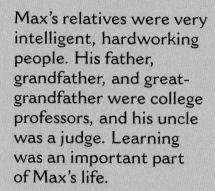

Planck read a great deal to learn from the work of other scientists.

Music or Science?

Max Planck studied science and math, but he was also a gifted musician. He was a talented singer and played the piano, organ, and cello. He even wrote songs and operas. Planck thought about having a career in music, but science won out. He gave up his formal study of music to focus on physics instead. But music always played an important part in his life.

When Max was 9 years old, his family moved to Munich, Germany, where a teacher named Hermann Müller took Max under his wing. He taught the boy math as well as mechanics and astronomy. It was from Müller that Max first became interested in energy and learned that it cannot be created or destroyed. Max enjoyed school and studied hard. He graduated early, at the age of 16.

But there was one cloud over Max's childhood. One of his earliest memories was of war. Troops marched through his hometown when he was a young boy, during the German-Danish War of 1864. War was common during Max's childhood. It would also become a tragic part of his adulthood as he lived through World War I and World War II.

Planck and his family moved to Munich in 1867.

At the age of 17, Max Planck enrolled at the University of Munich. Although his professor discouraged his interest, he decided to study physics and learn what scientists had already discovered in that field. He performed the same experiments others had already done. But the more he learned, the more he thought about what else could be uncovered.

In 1877, at the age of 19, Planck transferred to the University of Berlin. He studied for a year under two famous scientists and a mathematician. There he began to study theories of physics. Theories are explanations of how things work or why things happen. They are ways to try to understand what cannot be seen or what has not yet been proved. Planck, now called a theoretical physicist, soon proved that there were, in fact, new things to learn about science.

Physics Hall at the University of Munich

Planck focused first on heat and its properties. His curious mind led him to discover new things about what happens to matter, heat, and energy under various conditions. What he studied is a branch of physics called thermodynamics. Planck would go on to make many important discoveries in the field of thermodynamics.

From Newton to New Ideas

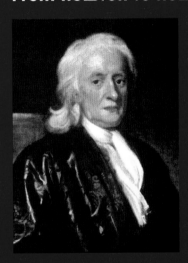

Isaac Newton (1642–1727) is one of the most important scientists of all time. Although he lived and studied 200 years before Planck, Newton's work was the foundation for Planck's theories. Newton was a great English physicist, mathematician, and astronomer. Many people think of him as the founder of modern physical science. His theory on gravity and motion is said to be the greatest work in the history of science. He also developed significant theories on color, light, and sound.

Newton's work was the basis for many great scientific discoveries. His theories are still important to scientists today. Newton was so well respected that scientists during Planck's time thought Newton had figured everything out about Earth and the universe. But Planck and other scientists through the years proved that there is always more to learn when it comes to science.

Professor Planck

By 1880, at the age of 22, Max Planck had received the two highest academic degrees offered in Europe. First he received a doctorate for his paper outlining his research and findings on his theory of thermodynamics. Then he wrote a second paper about another characteristic of heat. For that he received a habilitation, a degree that recognizes the highest level of academic achievement.

For five years, Planck lectured on his ideas without getting paid. In 1885, he got a job as a physics professor at the University of Kiel in his hometown. Four years later, one of Planck's former college professors died, and Planck replaced him at the University of Berlin.

Another Great Physicist

Albert Einstein was born in 1879, the year Planck received his doctoral degree from the University of Berlin. Einstein's research and theories on matter and energy would become some of the most important ideas in the history of physics. He had a remarkable ability to understand how the universe works. Einstein is best known for his theory of relativity and his formula $E=mc^2$. Einstein's formula means that a very small piece of matter can release an incredible amount of energy. When people think of Einstein, they usually think of "genius" and $E=mc^2$. Planck supported Einstein's theory of relativity and encouraged other scientists to accept it.

Planck's classroom was packed with students who were eager to hear this professor's new ideas about thermodynamics.

In 1887, during his years at Kiel, Planck had married Marie Merck, the sister of one of his schoolmates. The couple would eventually have two sons and twin daughters. Their home became a gathering place for other great scientists and thinkers. People came there to talk as well as listen to music and play their instruments. Like Planck, many of his scientist friends took great pleasure in music.

While Planck taught college courses, he continued to study thermodynamics. He knew that heat doesn't stay in one place. It moves around, passing from one piece of matter to another. Matter is anything that takes up space or has mass. All matter is made up of tiny particles called atoms, which can be seen only through a powerful microscope. How atoms join together is what makes matter unique. And how the atoms move has a lot to do with heat and energy. Planck's ideas about heat were based on a simple concept, but what he found was very significant.

Zeroth Law

There are four laws of thermodynamics: the first, second, third, and zeroth. The zeroth law was added after the others. It was a basic idea—that heat only goes from hot things to cooler things. Since it was so obvious, scientists had not included it in the laws of thermodynamics. In the early 1900s, however, they decided to add it to the laws. It was basic, so it should come first. But there was already a first law of thermodynamics. So scientists gave this one the number zero—and called it the zeroth law of thermodynamics.

Planck explained that at very high temperatures, the temperature of a substance can be estimated by its color. Beginning at about 525 degrees Fahrenheit (274 degrees Celsius), all substances begin to glow. As the temperature increases, the glow changes from red to yellow to white to blue. For example, lava that reaches temperatures as high as 2,200 F (1,204 C) appears bright red and yellow with patches of white.

Planck also studied how heat moves in three ways—conduction, convection, and radiation.

Conduction happens when vibrating atoms pass heat to each other. Convection happens when warm material moves to a cooler material and takes heat with it. Radiation happens when a substance naturally gives off energy. For example, the light and heat from the sun is radiation. Its energy moves in rays or waves.

In Planck's time, people knew about the first two types of heat movement. But they didn't know much about the third. Planck explained what radiation is and how it provides energy.

Seeing in the Dark

Objects naturally give off heat waves, or radiation. Special cameras with infrared sensors can take pictures of things in the dark because they detect the heat waves. Objects

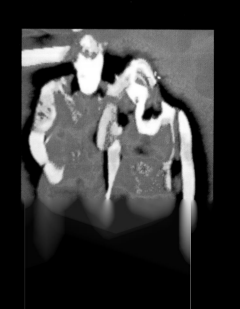

Marie Curie (1867—1934)

Another scientist interested in energy and matter, and especially radiation, was Marie Curie of Poland and France. In her time, it was rare for women to study science and math. Like most early female scientists, she was married to a scientist. Marie and her husband, Pierre Curie, worked endless hours experimenting with substances that gave off natural energy. She called this energy radioactivity. Certain substances such as radium and plutonium give off large amounts of radioactive energy. Radioactivity happens when the nucleus of an atom breaks down during decay. The atoms give off energy in the form of tiny radioactive particles.

Marie and Pierre Curie won a Nobel Prize in 1903 for their work on radioactive substances. Marie went on to win another Nobel Prize in 1911. The Nobel Prize consists of six awards given yearly for outstanding achievement in the areas of physics, chemistry, physiology or medicine, literature, economics, and world peace. Marie was the first woman to win a Nobel Prize. But the Curies were too sick to travel to Sweden to accept the award. The radioactive elements they had handled over the years had given them cancer. In the late 1920s, scientists who studied radioactive matter began protecting themselves from these harmful particles.

Curie's work was important to scientists such as Planck who studied energy and matter. Scientists continue to build on the work that Marie Curie began. Today radioactive elements are used in nuclear power stations to provide energy. Radiation is also used to treat cancer and kill harmful organisms in food.

Marie Curie died of cancer on July 4, 1934, at the age of 66. She sacrificed her health for her work. But what she discovered changed science and changed the world and the way it views matter and energy.

Entropy—How Atoms Are Ordered

To understand heat, Planck needed to know more than just how it moves. One of the things he studied was entropy, an idea that became very important to his theories.

Entropy is the randomness, or "messiness," of the atoms in a system. In a system with high entropy, there is no order to the atoms. High entropy is something like a messy bedroom.

For example, if all your belongings are thrown all over your room, there is high entropy, or no order. Items are strewn about at random. In a system with low entropy, atoms are orderly. This is like a bedroom that is tidy, with everything in a place that makes sense. Clothes are in the closet. Books are stacked neatly on the shelves. Things are in order, and there is a low level of randomness, or low entropy.

The Energy in Light

Light is a wave that carries energy. Each color in light has a different energy. Planck showed how to figure the energy carried by colors of light. He did this by linking light waves to entropy, or how ordered the atoms are in each color.

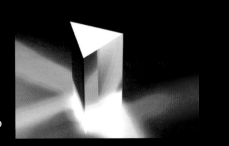

Did You Know?

According to the second law of thermodynamics, heat and energy will move around until things are as disordered as possible.

Heat Death of the Universe

There is a fixed amount of energy in the universe. New energy is not created, and the energy that exists does not leave or get used up. Energy just moves around from place to place. Some scientists believe that because atoms always move toward entropy (according to the second law of thermodynamics), there should be a point where entropy is as high as it can get. At this point, the universe would be a complete mess. There would be no more movement and no more energy. They believe that the universe will someday run down and be completely at rest, or "dead." This theory is called the heat death of the universe. Nobody knows if heat death will happen. Many scientists believe that entropy will just continue to increase forever.

Another example of entropy is a new deck of playing cards. The cards start out in a condition of low entropy—arranged in order according to suit and number. Once they are shuffled, however, they become a high-entropy system, with the cards in random order.

In order for entropy to go down, or become more ordered, a lot of energy is needed. Just as it takes a lot of energy to clean a very messy room, it takes a lot of energy to bring order to atoms. The more random the mess, the more energy it takes to clean it up.

Did You Know?

The word *entropy* comes from a Greek word meaning "turning toward." It has come to be used in fields other than thermodynamics to describe a disordered state.

Shuffling an ordered deck of playing cards turns a ⬆ low-entropy system into a high-entropy system.

Stephen Hawking
(1942–   )

Stephen Hawking is a theoretical physicist, following in the footsteps of Planck. Hawking was born in England in 1942, the year Planck turned 82 years old. Hawking began studying physics at an early age. After receiving a doctoral degree, he became a college professor. Like Planck, Hawking has spent his entire life studying the basic laws that govern the universe.

Hawking holds a position of great honor at Cambridge University in Oxford, England. It is called the Lucasian Professor of Mathematics. The post was founded in 1663. In 1669, it was given to the great scientist and mathematician Isaac Newton. Hawking has held the position since 1979.

Hawking has built on the work of great physicists such as Planck, Newton, and Einstein. He has developed new theories about the nature of black holes, as well as how our universe began. In 1988, he wrote a book, *A Brief History of Time,* about his theories. It remained on a British bestseller list for more than four years.

Since his college days, Hawking has had a disease called amyotrophic lateral sclerosis (ALS), often called Lou Gehrig's disease. The disease progressively gets worse, severely restricting Hawking's movements and speech. He communicates with a special device that can either print or speak his words. He jokes that his only regret is that the device has an American accent.

Planck's study of entropy led him to a new idea in 1900 that came to be called the quantum theory. This theory was Planck's greatest discovery, and it changed the way scientists understood energy. Planck explained that energy was contained in quanta, tiny units or packets of energy. For example, light appears to be a continuous wave of energy. But it is actually a collection of subatomic packets called quanta. One particle of subatomic energy is called a quantum.

Planck's theory changed the way physicists thought about energy. For years, the laws of physics had explained energy and how things moved. But they hadn't explained how things were moving about inside atoms. The quantum theory did just that.

Quantum Creations

It's easier to understand how things move and act when we can see them. The laws of physics tell us why these things behave the way they do. But without a very powerful microscope, we cannot see quanta, the tiny particles of energy inside the atom. Quanta can move however they want, and sometimes they don't follow the rules. They are just like small children: If you can't see them, they are likely to do something you don't expect.

Scientists are still studying how things work on this very small scale. What they learn will help scientists make amazing things such as more powerful computers. Scientists are working now to make computers that act like quanta. These computers will store information in what they call quantum binary digits, or qubits for short. Huge amounts of information will be able to be stored and retrieved in an instant.

Planck's quantum theory explained how tiny particles inside atoms, such as electrons, move about. The theory also explained why some things are radioactive. Radioactivity happens when the nucleus, or core, of some atoms breaks down during decay, releasing subatomic energy from inside the atoms. This release of energy is called radioactivity.

Planck's Constant

Planck based his quantum theory on a scientific formula. The most important part of his formula was the "h"—which stood for the size of the quanta. It was the unchangeable, or constant, part of the formula. It came to be called Planck's constant. Planck's formula can be found on his tombstone in Germany. It reads: $h = 6.626 \times 10^{-34}$ joule-seconds (j-s).

Scientists have used quantum theory to "teleport" information from one place to another instantly. Someday you may even be able to teleport yourself from one place to another!

Quantum Theory and the Speed of Light

Planck's quantum theory helped scientists figure out something that had been puzzling them since 1887. That year, two scientists showed that light waves travel at the same speed everywhere all the time. This didn't make sense to people. They expected light to travel faster if the source of the light were moving toward them.

After Planck introduced his quantum theory, scientists were able to explain why light always travels at a constant speed. The quantum theory continues to help today's scientists understand how energy works.

No matter how fast cars go, the light from their headlights still travels at the same speed.

Lasers and Quanta

Normal light from the sun or a lightbulb is made up of a variety of colors. The light and colors spread out over a wide area, sending color in all directions. Light from a laser is different. Lasers are based on the quantum theory. A laser separates the quanta in light and uses just one color. Because those quanta are all lined up in the same direction, they don't spread out.

Laser light is made by forcing electrons inside atoms to give out a certain type and number of quanta. That is why the light from one type of laser is always the same color. Lasers were invented 40 years after Planck explained his quantum theory. The theory made it possible to make lasers, which now have many uses in our everyday lives. They read information from a CD or DVD by scanning the surface of a disc with light. Lasers read bar codes at checkout counters and print documents from a computer. They are used to make holograms or perform surgeries. What other things do you think will be invented using the ideas of Planck's quantum theory?

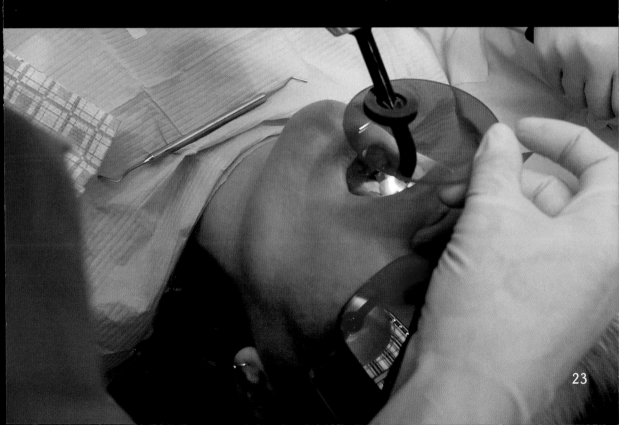

The first 50 years of Max Planck's life were good to him. He had experienced a happy childhood and interesting college years, and he had a family of his own. He enjoyed his friends and entertained often in his home. But beginning in 1909 a series of disasters struck. That year, his wife, Marie, died. They had been married for 22 years. In 1911, Planck married her cousin, Marga von Hoesslin. Together they had one son, Hermann.

In 1914, World War I began. That year, Planck's second son, Erwin, was taken prisoner. In 1916, his oldest son, Karl, was killed in battle. The following year, Margarete, one of his twin daughters, died giving birth to her first child. Two years later, his other daughter, Emma, also died in childbirth.

The war years were difficult ones, and Planck found it a challenge to continue his work. Even after the war

Soldiers and Red Cross aides in one of the many trenches that were common during World War I

ended in 1918, it was hard for scientists to concentrate on their research. Planck tried to encourage other scientists and came up with a slogan: "Persevere and continue working." He knew that his work and theirs was important and their discoveries would make the world a better place.

In 1933, life grew even harder for Planck and other scientists. The Nazi Party, headed by Adolf Hitler, took over Germany. Many great Jewish scientists were not allowed to work. Some were sent to prison. Although Planck was not Jewish, he argued that these scientists should be freed. His support for them cost him a very important job.

Planck traveled regularly in the 1930s, teaching and lecturing about his work and ideas. During this time, he gave a famous speech on religion and science. He was a devoted Christian and believed that both religion and science require a belief in God.

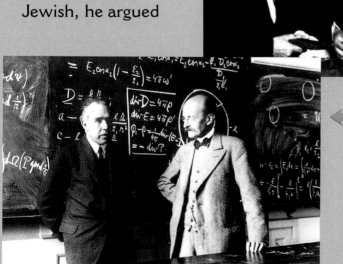

Planck with fellow scientists Albert Einstein (above) and Niels Bohr

In 1944, during World War II, more tragedies struck Planck. Bombs destroyed his home in Berlin. All of his science records were lost. That year, his son Erwin was arrested for his involvement in a plot to kill Hitler. The following year, Erwin died a terrible death at the hands of the Gestapo, the Nazi secret police.

The war ended in 1945, but it had taken its toll on Planck. With his second wife and only surviving child, he went to live with a relative in Göttingen, Germany. There, on October 4, 1947, Max Planck died after suffering multiple strokes. He was 89 years old.

But Planck left the world with part of himself—his ideas. The man who refused to believe that science was done gave the world new scientific theories and formulas. His discoveries changed forever the way we view our planet and our universe.

⬆ Many buildings were destroyed in bombing raids during World War II.

Sally Ride (1951—   )

In 1951, four years after the death of the great physicist Max Planck, Sally Ride was born in Los Angeles, California. She would study physics in college and then go on to be the first American woman to travel into outer space.

As a young girl, Ride enjoyed science, and her parents encouraged her interest in it. She grew up playing with a chemistry set and a simple telescope. She also played sports and competed in national junior tennis tournaments.

In college Ride studied physics and continued playing competitive tennis. She received her bachelor's, master's, and doctoral degrees from Stanford University in Palo Alto, California. In the late 1970s, Ride responded to an ad in the school newspaper announcing that NASA was accepting applications for astronauts. For the first time, NASA was also accepting women into the space program. Nearly 9,000 people applied. Ride was one of 35 (including five other women) who were accepted.

In 1983, Sally Ride became the first American woman to fly in space.

During her historic flight aboard the space shuttle *Challenger*, she deployed communications satellites, operated the robotic arm, and conducted experiments. Ride made her second trip into space one year later.

After leaving NASA Ride became a professor of physics at the University of California, San Diego. In 2001, she started her own company, Sally Ride Science, to pursue her longtime passion to motivate young people, especially girls, to pursue their interests in science.

Ride is best known as America's first woman in space. But among her most important work may be her inspiration to young people to follow their dreams—just as she followed hers.

Physicist: Frances Hellman

University of California, Berkeley

Physicists study and experiment with many things. Planck was interested in heat, while Einstein was fascinated with light. Physicist Frances Hellman is interested in new types of magnets.

Magnets are everywhere. They're in compasses, on refrigerators, and inside DVD players. But Hellman's magnets are special. She often builds them one atom at a time. Someday her new magnets might make batteries in an iPod last longer or allow you to put more games on a computer. "A lot of

In the future NASA might use magnetic tracks to launch spacecraft.

Hellman says ...

"Scientists come in all personality types." What's your personality type? Ask your friends, too!

people think of scientists as just sitting around thinking all the time," Hellman says. But scientists like Hellman build things. She adds, "It's not all pens and pencils and paper. It's very hands-on."

Hellman says all scientists are very curious people. According to Hellman, a good scientist is "somebody who looks around and says, 'Gee, I wonder why the sky is blue,' instead of just accepting that the sky is blue."

Think About It

Hellman likes to design new materials that can be used in new products. Can you think of a new product that would make your life easier or more interesting? What material could you design that would be in that product?

Materials Science

A materials scientist creates new materials such as plastics and metals. If you were a materials scientist, you might ...

- make airplanes stronger and lighter

- make computers faster and smaller

- make new body parts for people who are ill or disabled

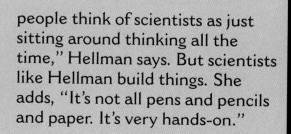

Name:	Max Planck
Date of birth:	April 23, 1858
Nationality:	German
Birthplace:	Kiel, Germany
Parents:	Johann Julius Wilhelm Planck and Emma Patzig Planck
Spouses:	Marie Merck (1861–1909) Marga von Hoesslin (1882–1948)
Children:	With Marie Merck: Karl (1888–1916); Margarete (1889–1917); Emma (1889–1919); Erwin (1893–1945) With Marga von Hoesslin: Hermann (1911–1954)
Date of death:	October 4, 1947
Field of study:	Physics
Known for:	Quantum theory
Contributions to science:	Planck's constant, quantum theory
Awards and honors:	Nobel Prize in physics, 1918; Lorentz Medal, 1927; Max Planck Medal, 1929; Copley Medal, 1929; honorary doctorates from the universities of Frankfurt, Munich, Rostock, Berlin, Graz, Athens, Cambridge, London, and Glasgow; asteroid 1069 named "Stella Planckia" in his honor in 1938

The Work of Max Planck

1858	Max Planck is born April 23
1875	Attends the University of Munich; studies physics despite the discouragement of his professor
1877	Attends the University of Berlin; studies physics under two famous scientists and a mathematician
1879	Receives a doctorate in physics from the University of Berlin
1885	Becomes a physics professor at the University of Kiel
1887	Marries Marie Merck in March
1888	Son Karl is born
1889	Becomes a physics professor at the University of Berlin; twin daughters, Margarete and Emma, are born
1893	Son Erwin is born
1900	States his quantum theory, explaining quanta, the tiny subatomic packets of energy
1909	Wife, Marie, dies
1911	Marries Marga von Hoesslin in March; son Hermann is born in December

1914	World War I begins; his second son, Erwin, is taken prisoner
1916	Oldest son, Karl, is killed in battle
1917	Daughter Margarete dies giving birth to her first child; the child survives
1919	Daughter Emma also dies in childbirth; her child also survives
1933	The Nazi Party takes over Germany; Jewish scientists are not allowed to work or are sent to prison; Planck argues that these scientists should be freed
1944	Bombs destroy Planck's home in Berlin, destroying all his science records; son Erwin is arrested for his involvement in a failed attempt to assassinate Adolf Hitler, the Nazi dictator of Germany
1945	Son Erwin is hanged by the Nazis on January 23 for his participation in the failed attempt to assassinate Hitler; Planck, his second wife, and only surviving child, Hermann, go to live with a relative in Göttingen, Germany
1947	Dies in Göttingen October 4 at the age of 89 after suffering multiple strokes

André Marie Ampère (1911–1988)
French physicist and mathematician who laid
the foundation of the science of electrodynamics
and determined that electric currents produce
magnetic fields

Antoine Henri Becquerel (1852–1908)
French physicist who discovered radioactivity by
accident in 1896 when a piece of uranium left in a dark
desk drawer made an image on photographic plates

Niels Bohr (1885–1962)
Danish physicist who received the Nobel Prize in
physics in 1922 for his contribution to understanding
the structure of atoms that are made up of protons,
neutrons, and electrons

Max Born (1882–1970)
German-born British physicist who is known for
his work on the probability interpretation of
quantum mechanics

Irène Joliot-Curie (1897–1956)
French chemist and daughter of Marie and Pierre
Curie, who, together with her husband, received the
Nobel Prize in chemistry in 1935 for the discovery of
artificial radioactivity

Marie Sklodowska-Curie (1867–1934)
Polish/French physicist and chemist who was awarded
two Nobel Prizes (1906 and 1911) for her pioneering
work in radioactivity

Pierre Curie (1859–1906)
French physicist who shared the Nobel Prize with his
wife, Marie Curie, in 1903 for their research on radiation

John Dalton (1766–1844)
English chemist and physicist best known for developing
the atomic theory

Albert Einstein (1879–1955)
German/American physicist best known for his theory of relativity and specifically mass-energy equivalence ($E=mc^2$).

Michael Faraday (1791–1867)
British physicist and chemist who proposed the idea of magnetic "lines of force," developed the first electric generator, and pioneered the study of low temperatures

Werner Heisenberg (1901–1976)
German physicist who developed the Uncertainty Principle, which advanced modern physics; realized that the atomic nucleus consisted of protons and neutrons; won the Nobel Prize in 1932

James Joule (1818–1889)
British physicist who determined the amount of heat produced by an electric current (named joule in his honor); determined that if a gas expands without performing work, its temperature falls

Ernst Mach (1838–1916)
Austrian physicist who discovered that airflow becomes disturbed at the speed of sound; mach numbers, which represent how fast a craft is traveling beyond the speed of sound, were named after him

James Maxwell (1831–1879)
British physicist who developed equations that served as a basis for the understanding of electromagnetism; determined that light is electromagnetic radiation and predicted other types of radiation beyond visible light; developed the kinetic theory of gases, a foundation of modern physical chemistry

Maria Goeppert-Mayer (1906–1972)
American physicist known for her research on the nucleus of an atom; received the Nobel Prize in physics in 1963, becoming the second woman to receive the award (Marie Curie was the first)

Dimitri Ivanovich Mendeleev (1834–1907)
Russian chemist credited with creating the first version
of the periodic table of the elements

Albert Michelson (1852–1931)
American physicist who accurately determined the
speed of light, accurate to within several thousandths
of a percent; along with Edward Morley, invented the
interferometer to show that light travels at a constant
velocity, regardless of the movement of Earth, an idea
that eventually led to Einstein's theory of relativity

Edward Morley (1838–1923)
American chemist and physicist who, along with Albert
Michelson, developed the interferometer to show that
the velocity of light is a constant (called the Michelson-
Morley experiment)

Isaac Newton (1643–1727)
English physicist and mathematician who was one of
the greatest scientists of all time; invented calculus,
determined the nature of white light, constructed the
first reflecting telescope, and formulated the laws of
motion and the theory of universal gravitation

J. Robert Oppenheimer (1904–1967)
American physicist who, along with his work in
astrophysics, was the director of the Manhattan
Project to build the first atomic bomb

Wilhelm Conrad Röntgen (1845–1923)
German physicist who discovered X-rays in 1895

Ernest Rutherford (1871–1937)
English physicist who studied the element uranium and
became known as the father of nuclear physics

Joseph John Thomson (1856–1940)
English physicist known for the discoveries of the
electron and isotopes; received the Nobel Prize in
physics in 1906

Glossary

atom—smallest particle of an element

conduction—passing of heat between moving particles

convection—movement of warm material to a cooler area, taking heat with it

energy—power to do work

entropy—measure of disorder in a system

infrared—electromagnetic radiation often associated with heat

laser—device that generates a beam of light of the same color moving in the same direction; produced by forcing electrons to emit a set number of quanta

matter—particles of which everything in the universe is made

physics—science that studies matter, energy, force, and motion

quantum—subatomic packet of energy (plural: quanta)

quantum theory—explanation of how things behave on a very small scale (atomic and subatomic); theory states that energy is transmitted in units called quanta

radiation—transfer of heat by waves or particles

radioactivity—process of giving off energy as a substance's atomic nuclei break down

subatomic—relating to particles that are smaller than an atom

theory—idea, explanation, or principle

thermodynamics—study of the movement of heat

Fleisher, Paul. *Relativity and Quantum Mechanics: Principles of Modern Physics*. New York: Lerner Publications, 2001.

Fortey, Jacqueline. *Great Scientists*. London: DK, 2007.

Leiter, Darryl J., and Sharon L. Leiter. *A to Z of Physicists*. Facts on File, 2003.

Rosinsky, Natalie M. *Sir Isaac Newton: Brilliant Mathematician and Scientist*. Minneapolis: Compass Point Books, 2008.

Solway, Andrew. *A History of Super Science*. Chicago: Raintree, 2006.

Whiting, Jim. *John Dalton and the Atomic Theory*. Hockessin, Del.: Mitchell Lane Publishers, 2005.

On the Web

For more information on this topic, use FactHound.

1. Go to *www.facthound.com*
2. Choose your grade level.
3. Begin your search.

This book's ID number is 9780756540739

FactHound will find the best sites for you.

Index

Jane Weir

Jane Weir grew up in Leicester, England. She graduated from the University of Sheffield with a master's degree in physics and astronomy, but gained much of her practical knowledge of physics through rock-climbing. Weir currently lives in Salisbury, England, where she works as a scientist for the British government.

Image Credits

FEB 2010